Amateur Wine Lover's Quiz Book

A - Z of Wines

Author Val Policella

ISBN: 1978096968
ISBN-13: 978-1978096967

Amateur Wine Lover's Quiz Book

CONTENTS

Introduction

This book is a collection of quiz questions for amateur wine enthusiasts designed to test your knowledge of wines and wine related trivia of various wines.

Some of the wines are varietal wines and some blends. A varietal wine is a wine primarily produced from a single grape variety. A blend consists of two or more grape varieties.

I have had several great evenings with family and friends over the years whilst sharing a fabulous bottle of wine or two!

Why not open a bottle or two with friends and family or host your own wine evening, pick up this quiz book, put your quizmaster's hat on and away you go.

I hope you enjoy these quizzes as much as I have.

Amateur Wine Lover's Quiz Book

ALBARIÑO

1. The Albariño grape is a white wine grape grown in Spain and Portugal. What is it called in Portugal?

2. This grape variety typically produces wines of which alcohol level?

    A. 9.5-12%

    B. 10-11%

    C. 11.5-12.5%

3. True or false? Albariño is also produced in California.

4. Albariño wines have a distinct aroma of which fruits?

5. True or false? In 2008 it was discovered that Australian wine producers have been selling French Savagnin as Albariño.

ALIGOTÉ

1. The Aligoté grape is used to make which type of wine?

    A. White wine

    B. Red wine

    C. Sparkling wine

2. Aligoté wine was 1st recorded in the Burgundy wine region of France in which century?

    A. 17th

    B. 18th

    C. 19th

3. True or false? The Aligoté grape originates from Portugal.

4. In the Burgundy region how does the Aligoté grape rank for popularity of growth after Chardonnay?

A. 2nd

B. 4th

C. 5th

5. Aligoté wines have the aroma of which fruits?

A. Oranges and Lemons

B. Pineapple and Grapefruit

C. Apples and Lemons

AMARONE

1. What is the full name of Amarone wine?

2. Which type of rich Italian wine is Amarone?

    A. Sparkling wine

    B. Dessert wine

    C. Red wine

3. What is the legal minimum level of alcohol required for Amarone wine?

    A. 13%

    B. 14%

    C. 15%

4. True or false? Twice as many grapes are used to produce Amarone wine as used in other wines.

5. What does Amarone mean in Italian?

ARNEIS

1. Which Italian wine region does Arneis originate from?

2. Which type of wine is produced from the Arneis grape?

   A. Red wine

   B. Dessert wine

   C. White wine

3. Which style do these wines tend to be?

   A. Dry and full bodied

   B. Sweet and medium bodied

   C. Dry and light bodied

4. In New Zealand the Arneis grape variety is mostly found in which region?

   A. Nelson

   B. Central Otago

   C. Gisborne

5. Classic flavor notes and aromas for Arneis wines are?

   A. Citrus

   B. Pears and apricots

   C. Apples and pears

ASTI SPUMANTE

1. Which type of wine is Asti Spumante?

   A. White wine

   B. Sparkling wine

   C. Dessert wine

2. Asti Spumante production is mainly focused around the towns of Asti and Alba. Which Italian wine region are these towns located in?

3. Which grape variety is used for producing Asti Spumante?

   A. Moscato Bianco

   B. Albaranzeuli Bianco

   C. Bianco d'Alessano

4. Is Asti Spumante a varietal or blended wine?

5. What level of alcohol does Asti

Spumante have?

A. 7-9.5%

B. 8-10%

C. 9-11.5%

AUSLESE

1. What does Auslese translate as?

    A. Late harvest

    B. Selected harvest

    C. Harvest

2. Auslese wines are often considered which type of German wine?

    A. Fortified wine

    B. Ice wine

    C. Dessert wine

3. Auslese wines typically have which level of alcohol content?

    A. 9-11%

    B. 11-13%

    C. 13-14%

4. When Auslese wines are made from

Riesling grapes they can often be aged for how long?

A. 3-5 years

B. 5-7 years

C. 10 years or more

5. What is the minimum level of alcohol content for Auslese wines?

A. 7%

B. 10%

C. 11%

BANYULS

1. Which type of wine is Banyuls wine?

   A. Dessert wine

   B. Red wine

   C. White wine

2. What is the minimum level of alcohol content required by law for Banyuls wine?

   A. 11%

   B. 14%

   C. 15%

3. What is the minimum maturation period for Banyuls wine?

   A. 10 months

   B. 18 months

   C. 36 months

4. Is a Banyuls wine varietal or blended?

5. True or false? A typical Banyuls wine is full bodied with raspberry, blackcurrant and vanilla flavours.

BARBARESCO

1. The vineyards around the town of Barbaresco account for how much of the total production of Barbaresco wine?

   A. 45%

   B. 60%

   C. 70%

2. Barbaresco wines must have a minimum alcohol content of how much?

   A. 10%

   B. 11%

   C. 12.5%

3. Is Barbaresco wine varietal or blended wine?

4. What is the minimum time a Barbaresco wine must be aged before it

can be released?

A. 2 years (1 in oak)

B. 3 years (2 in oak)

C. 4 years (3 in oak)

5. What are 2 of the flavor notes of a typical Barbaresco wine?

A. Raspberry and vanilla

B. Blackcurrant and chocolate

C. Cherry and licorice

BARDOLINO

1. Which type of wine is a Bardolino wine?

   A. Sparkling wine

   B. White wine

   C. Red wine

2. The Bardolino wine is a blended wine which primarily consists of Corvina, Rondinella and which other grape variety?

   A. Molinara

   B. Sangiovese

   C. Nebbiolo

3. Bardolino wine is produced in which Italian wine region?

   A. Veneto

   B. Abruzzo

C. Calabria

4. True or false? Bardolino Novello is produced in a style which mimics Beaujolais Nouveau.

5. Other than the 3 main grape varieties additional grape blending is allowed up to how much of the total?

A. 12%

B. 15%

C. 26%

BAROLO

1. Which grape variety is used to produce Barolo wine?

   A. Nebbiolo

   B. Dolcetto

   C. Pavia

2. What is the minimum alcohol content required for a Barolo wine?

   A. 12.5%

   B. 13%

   C. 14%

3. How long must a Barolo wine be aged before it can be labelled "Riserva"?

   A. 36 months (18 months in oak)

   B. 48 months (18months in oak)

   C. 60 months (18 months in oak)

4. Are Barolo wines typically light, medium or full bodied?

5. True or false? The after dinner digestif named Barolo Chinato is made from the bark of the Eucalyptus tree steeped in Barolo.

BEAUJOLAIS

1. True or false? Beaujolais Nouveau is only allowed to be made from the Gamay grape.

2. White wines produced in the Beaujolais region account for how much of the wine production?

   A. 1%

   B. 5%

   C. 10%

3. In the Beaujolais region, which grape is mostly used for white wine production?

   A. Ugni Blanc

   B. Sauvignon Blanc

   C. Chardonnay

4. True or false? Beaujolais Nouveau is always released on the 2nd Thursday in November.

5. How much of the entire crop grown in the Beaujolais region is sold as Beaujolais Nouveau?

A. 1/3

B. 1/4

C. 2/3

BRUNELLO di MONTALCINO

1. True or false? Brunello di Montalcino is a varietal wine and can only be made using 100% Sangiovese grapes.

2. Which Italian wine region is Brunello di Montalcino wine from?

   A. Abruzzo

   B. Lombardy

   C. Tuscany

3. Which type of wine is Brunello di Montalcino?

   A. Red wine

   B. White wine

   C. Sparkling wine

4. What is the minimum time of ageing required before Brunello di Montalcino

can be released for sale?

A. 1 year in a barrel and 1 year in the bottle

B. 2 years in a barrel and 4 months in the bottle

C. 5 years in a barrel and 6 months in the bottle

5. Is Brunello di Montalcino light, medium or full bodied?

CABERNET FRANC

1. True or false? Cabernet Franc grapes are used for varietal and blended wines.

2. In Washington State USA, how does the Cabernet Franc rank for most planted?

    A. 2nd

    B. 3rd

    C. 4th

3. True or false? In Canada Cabernet Franc is now being used to produce Ice wine?

4. Cabernet Franc wines produced in Hungary is typically aged in oak barrels for how long?

    A. 12-18 months

    B. 18-24 months

    C. 24-36 months

5. True or false? Cabernet Franc and Savagnin Blanc are the "parents" of Cabernet Sauvignon.

CABERNET SAUVIGNON

1. Is the classic Cabernet Sauvignon light, medium or full bodied?

2. True or false? Cabernet Sauvignon is usually aged in oak for at least 24 months.

3. How much alcohol content does a Cabernet Sauvignon typically have?

    A. 11-13%

    B. 12-14%

    C. 13.5-15.5%

4. The Bordeaux wine region accounts for how much of the Cabernet Sauvignon grown in France?

    A. 60%

    B. 70%

    C. 80%

5. True or false? Cabernet Sauvignon grapes tend to produce wines with blackcurrant and black cherry notes, however, in the Coonawarra region of Australia wines tend to have eucalyptus or menthol notes.

CARMÉNÈRE

1. True or false? The Carménère grape originates from the Bordeaux region in France.

2. The world's largest area planted with the Carménère grape is in which country?

   A. France

   B. Chile

   C. Italy

3. 100% Carménère wine generally have which fruit flavour combination?

   A. Raspberry and pomegranate

   B. Black cherry and blackberry

   C. Raspberry and cherry

4. True or false? In Chile a varietal Carménère wine is allowed to have up to 20% of other grape varieties blended

with it.

5. True or false? In 1990 an Italian winery bought cuttings that they thought were Cabernet Franc and only realized they were Carménère when they ripened earlier and had a different colour and taste!

CAVA

1. Which type of wine is Cava?

   A. Red wine

   B. White wine

   C. Sparkling wine

2. What is the minimum length of time a Cava must be aged before it can be labelled Gran Reserva?

3. What does Dulce mean on a bottle of Cava?

   A. Sweet

   B. Semi-dry

   C. Dry

4. True or false? Spanish wine producers adopted the name Cava in 1970 in reference to the underground cellars where the wines ferment and age in the bottle

5. Cava is made in several regions across Spain. Catalonia is one of these regions. How much of Spain's total Cava production comes from Catalonia?

A. 55%

B. 75%

C. 95%

CHAMPAGNE

1. A person who turns Champagne bottles during the production process is called a Champagne riddler. How many can they turn each day?

   A. Up to 10,000 bottles

   B. Up to 20,000 bottles

   C. Up to 50,000 bottles

2. Which white grape is primarily used for Champagne production?

   A. Chardonnay

   B. Sauvignon Blanc

   C. Chenin Blanc

3. True or false? There are approx. 49 million bubbles in a bottle of Champagne.

4. Which red wine grape varieties are used for Champagne production?

A. Mourvèdre and Cabernet Franc

B. Pinot Noir and Pinot Meunier

C. Gamay and Carignan

5. Which French term is used to describe Champagne made from 100% Chardonnay?

CHARDONNAY

1. Which type of wine is Chardonnay?

   A. Red wine

   B. Sparkling wine

   C. White wine

2. True or false? Chardonnay is the most widely planted white grape variety in France.

3. How much alcohol content does Chardonnay typically have?

   A. 10-12%

   B. 12-15%

   C. 11-14%

4. What temperature should Chardonnay be served at?

   A. 7 □C

   B. 8 □C

C. 9 □C

5. True or false? Chardonnay is the only grape variety allowed to be grown in the Chablis region of Burgundy.

CHÂTEAUNEUF-du-PAPE

1. Châteauneuf-du-Pape is produced in which wine region?

   A. Rhône

   B. Normandy

   C. Loire

2. True or false? Châteauneuf-du-Pape can be red and white wine.

3. Châteauneuf-du-Pape is a blended wine. 18 grape varieties are allowed to be used in any quantities to produce this wine, but which is the most dominant grape variety used?

   A. Roussanne

   B. Muscardin

   C. Grenache

4. Only 1 in every how many bottles of Châteauneuf-du-Pape wines produced

is white wine?

A. 10

B. 16

C. 25

5. What is the minimum level of alcohol content a Châteauneuf-du-Pape must have?

CHENIN BLANC

1. Chenin Blanc is planted widely around the world. True or false? Nearly twice as much Chenin Blanc is planted in South Africa as is planted in France.

2. Chenin Blanc is planted in several wine regions in France. In which region is this variety most planted?

   A. Loire

   B. Brittany

   C. Savoy

3. In South Africa, Chenin Blanc accounts for how much of the total vineyard plantings?

   A. 1/3

   B. 1/4

   C. 1/5

4. True or false? Chenin Blanc from the

Loire has notes of apple and greengage but Chenin Blanc from South Africa has notes of banana and pineapple.

5. True or false? Chenin Blanc is left on the vines longer and harvested later for making sparkling or dry wines.

CHIANTI

1. Which is the main grape variety used in the production of Chianti?

    A. Brachetto

    B. Sangiovese

    C. Pascale

2. How much of this grape variety (answer number 1) must the wine contain?

    A. 45-50%

    B. 50-70%

    C. 75-100%

3. At what temperature should Chianti be served?

    A. 15 ☐C

    B. 17 ☐C

    C. 18 ☐C

4. What is the minimum alcohol content required for a Chianti wine?

   A. 9.5%

   B. 10.5%

   C. 11.5%

5. Chianti is a province in which Italian wine region?

   A. Piedmont

   B. Tuscany

   C. Veneto

CONSTANTIA

1. Which type of wine is Constantia?

   A. Red wine

   B. White wine

   C. Dessert wine

2. Which country produces Constantia?

3. Which grape variety is used to make Contantia?

   A. Muscat Blanc à Petits Grains

   B. Muscadelle

   C. Sauvignon Blanc

4. True or false? Napoleon Bonaparte had 30 bottles a month shipped over to St Helena to ease his exile.

5. In which country does the grape used to produce this wine originate?

CORTESE

1. Cortese is an Italian wine grape variety predominantly grown in which wine region?

    A. Veneto

    B. Sardinia

    C. Piedmont

2. How is a Cortese wine best described?

    A. Light bodied

    B. Medium bodied

    C. Full bodied

3. Which type of wine is produced from the Cortese grape variety?

    A. Red wine

    B. White wine

    C. Sparkling wine

4. Cortese wines typically have notes of which fruit combination?

   A. Lime and greengage

   B. Pineapple and grapefruit

   C. Apple and pear

5. The wine's moderate acidity and light, crisp flavors pair well with which type of food?

   A. Chicken

   B. Vegetarian

   C. Fish

DOLCETTO

1. Dolcetto is an Italian grape variety. What does "dolcetto" mean in Italian?

2. Which type of wine is produced with the Dolcetto grape?

   A. Red wine

   B. Dessert wine

   C. Fortified wine

3. Dolcetto wines are well known for which flavours?

   A. Blackberry and raspberry

   B. Plums and chocolate

   C. Black cherry and liquorice

4. Dolcetto pairs well with which types of food?

   A. Bbq meats

   B. Pasta and pizza

C. Roast beef

5. A Dolcetto wine is produced as standard or superior. What is the minimum level of alcohol content for a superior wine?

A. 10.5%

B. 12%

C. 12.5%

DURIF

1. In which country did the Durif grape originate?

    A. Italy

    B. Spain

    C. France

2. True or false? In the USA the Durif is known as Petite Sirah.

3. Which type of wine is Durif?

    A. White wine

    B. Red wine

    C. Sparkling wine

4. True or false? The Durif grape was created and named after the creator, Dr Durif.

5. How much alcohol content does a Durif wine typically have?

A. 10-12%

B. 12.5-13.5%

C. 14-15%

EISWEIN

1. What type of wine is Eiswein (ice wine)?

   A. Red wine

   B. White wine

   C. Dessert wine

2. True or false? Eiswein was created in Germany in 1794 when a wine producer found his vines had frozen overnight and was forced to press frozen grapes or lose his entire crop.

3. True or false? Grapes used for Eiswein are machine harvested to speed up the process so that pressing can be carried out immediately.

4. Canada accounts for how much of the Ice wine produced in the world?

   A. 55%

B. 65%

C. 75%

5. In Germany Eiswein alcohol content can be as low as 6%. But in Canada, what level does it tend to be?

A. 6-9%

B. 7-10%

C. 8-13%

GAMAY

1. True or false? The full name of the Gamay grape variety is "Gamay Noir à Jus Blanc".

2. Wines made with the Gamay grape tend to be which type?

   A. Light bodied

   B. Medium bodied

   C. Full bodied

3. Which flavours do Gamay grape wines typically have?

   A. Blackberry and sour cherry

   B. Strawberry and raspberry

   C. Black cherry and liquorice

4. True or false? The Gamay grape originates from Switzerland.

5. Beaujolais nouveau produced from the

Gamay grape is best served at which temperature?

A. 13 □C

B. 14 □C

C. 15 □C

GATTINARA

1. Gattinara is which type of wine?

    A. White wine

    B. Dessert wine

    C. Red wine

2. Gattinara wines are any wines produced in the boundaries of the commune of Gattinara. In which wine region is Gattinara located?

    A. Piedmont

    B. Lombardy

    C. Liguria

3. The wine is primarily made from which grape variety?

    A. Primitivo

    B. Nebbiolo

    C. Sagrantino

4. What is the minimum amount of this grape variety (answer number 3) that Gattinara wine must contain?

   A. 70%

   B. 80%

   C. 90%

5. How long must a Gattinara Riserva be aged for?

   A. 2 years in oak barrels and 1 year in the bottle

   B. 2 years in oak barrels and 2 years in the bottle

   C. 2 years in oak barrels and 3 years in the bottle

GEWÜRZTRAMINER

1. True or false? The Gewürztraminer grape variety originates from Germany in the foothills of the Alps.

2. What is the 1ˢᵗ aroma you will come across in a glass of Gewürztraminer wine?

   A. Grapefruit

   B. Lychee

   C. Pineapple

3. Gewürztraminer is grown widely throughout Europe. In which French wine region is it the 2ⁿᵈ most widely planted variety?

   A. Alsace

   B. Savoy

   C. Loire

4. What is the best temperature to serve a

Gewürztraminer wine?

A. 4 □C

B. 5 □C

C. 6 □C

5. Gewürztraminer wines are best paired with which type of cuisine?

A. Bavarian cuisine

B. Asian cuisine

C. French cuisine

GRENACHE

1. The Grenache grape variety is most often used for blended wines. Which type of wine does the Grenache grape produce?

   A. Dessert wine

   B. Sparkling wine

   C. Red wine

2. The Grenache variety is often one of the last varieties to be harvested. Due to the long ripening process, Grenache based wines can typically has at least which level of alcohol content?

   A. At least 14%

   B. At least 15%

   C. At least 15.5%

3. True or false? Grenache is the most common grape variety in France.

4. In Sardinia what is Grenache called?

   A. Granaccia

   B. Cannonau

   C. Garnacha

5. True or false? International Grenache day occurs annually on the 3rd Friday of September.

LAMBRUSCO

1. Which type of wine is Lambrusco?

   A. Sparkling wine

   B. White wine

   C. Dessert wine

2. Supermarket style Lambrusco wines (commercially produced) tend to be a lower quality and on average contain which level of alcohol content?

   A. 4.5%

   B. 5.5%

   C. 6.5%

3. Unlike most Supermarkets style Lambrusco wines; "Real Lambrusco" typically contains which level of alcohol content?

   A. 8%

B. 9.5%

C. 11%

4. There are six commonly used varieties of the Lambrusco grape. True or false? Most Lambrusco wines are made from a single grape variety.

5. How is a dry Lambrusco labelled?

A. Dolce

B. Amabile

C. Secco

LIEBFRAUMILCH

1. Which type of wine is Liebfraumilch?

   A. White wine

   B. Red wine

   C. Sparkling wine

2. Liebfraumilch is a blended wine. True or false? To be labelled Liebfraumilch the wine has to be made from at least 70% of Riesling, Silvaner or Müller-Thurgau.

3. What does Liebfraumilch translate as from German to English?

4. What style of wine is Liebfraumilch?

   A. Dry

   B. Off dry

   C. Semi-sweet

5. True or false? The majority of

Liebfraumilch produced is for the German domestic market.

MADEIRA

1. What is the minimum length of time a
    Madeira wine must be aged before it
    can be classed as Vintage?

    A. 15 years

    B. 20 years

    C. 25 years

2. Which type of wine is Madeira?

    A. Red wine

    B. Fortified wine

    C. Rosé wine

3. True or false? A Madeira wine labelled
    as "Finest" is aged for 3 years and
    normally reserved for cooking.

4. There are 4 major styles of single
    varietal Madeira. Put these is order of
    driest to sweetest.

A. Verdelho

B. Malmsey

C. Bual

D. Sercial

5. Madeira wine gets its name from the Madeira Islands where it is produced. Situated in the North Atlantic Ocean, which European country does the Madeira Islands belong to?

MALBEC

1. Which type of wine is Malbec?

    A. Red wine

    B. Fortified wine

    C. Port style wine

2. The Malbec grape variety originates from France. True or false? These days Argentina accounts for 75% of Malbec grown in the world.

3. Which style of wine is Malbec?

    A. Light bodied

    B. Medium bodied

    C. Full bodied

4. At which temperature should Malbec be served?

    A. 18 ☐C

    B. 21 ☐C

C. 23 □C

5. What are the typical fruit flavour
    characteristics of Malbec wine?

    A. Black Cherry, Pomegranate, Plum

    B. Raspberry, Blackberry, Blueberry

    C. A + B

MARSALA

1. Marsala is a blended fortified wine. True or false? Marsala is only used as a cooking wine.

2. In which Italian wine region is Marsala wine produced?

   A. Sicily

   B. Calabria

   C. Veneto

3. A typical Marsala wine contains which level of alcohol?

   A. 9-14%

   B. 15-20%

   C. 20-22%

4. How long is "Superiore Riserva" Marsala is aged for?

   A. At least 4 years

B. At least 6 years

C. At least 10 years

5. The most common flavors of Marsala wine are vanilla, brown sugar, stewed apricot and tamarind. What is the best temperature to serve Marsala wine for best tasting results?

A. 11 □C

B. 12 □C

C. 13 □C

MARSANNE

1. Marsanne is a white wine grape variety. Which type of wine is produced from the Marsanne grape?

   A. Varietal

   B. Blended

   C. Varietal and blended

2. True or false? A wine made with Marsanne grapes typically has aromas of honeysuckle, pineapple and peach.

3. Where does the Marsanne grape originate from?

   A. France

   B. Switzerland

   C. Spain

4. Which styles of wines are made from Marsanne grapes?

A. Light bodied

B. Medium bodied

C. Full bodied

5. In Northern Rhône Marsanne tends to be blended with how much Rousanne grape variety to produce rich aromatic, nutty wines?

A. 10%

B. 15%

C. 20%

MERLOT

1. True or false? Merlot is the world's most planted wine grape variety.

2. True or false? Merlot is the most planted grape variety in France?

3. Which type of wine is Merlot?

    A. Fortified wine

    B. Red wine

    C. Dessert wine

4. True or false? In the 1990's, the Argentinian wine industry sold a large amount of wine made from the Carménerè grape as Merlot.

5. A typical Merlot wine has characteristics of with fruit?

    A. Black Cherry, Raspberry, Plum

    B. Blackcurrant, Black Cherry, Blueberry

C. Blueberry, Cherry, Blackberry

MOURVÈDRE

1. Mourvèdre is a red wine grape variety grown in various countries. Which country grows the most Mourvèdre?

    A. France

    B. Spain

    C. Australia

2. Which style of wine is Mourvèdre?

    A. Light bodied

    B. Medium bodied

    C. Full bodied

3. Mourvèdre is one of the grape varieties allowed to be blended in which famous wine produced in the Southern Rhône wine region of France?

4. True or false? Strawberry, Raspberry and Cherry are typical flavours of a

Mourvèdre wine.

5. True or false? As well as being used to produce blended red wine, Mourvèdre is used in Australia to produce Port style wines.

NEBBIOLO

1. Which country does the Nebbiolo grape originate from?

2. True or false? The Nebbiolo grape is the only grape variety allowed to be used for production of Barolo and Barbaresco wines.

3. Which style of wine is typically produced from Nebbiolo grapes?

    A. Light bodied

    B. Medium bodied

    C. Full bodied

4. In the Roero wine region in Italy. What is the minimum amount of Nebbiolo grapes that must be used to produce red wine?

    A. 75%

    B. 85%

C. 95%

5. What is the minimum length of time that a Roero wine must be aged?

   A. 20 months (6 months in wooden barrels)

   B. 30 months (6 months in wooden barrels)

   C. 40 months (6 months in wooden barrels)

PETIT VERDOT

1. True or false? Petit Verdot is a red wine
    grape principally used in classic
    Bordeaux blends to add colour.

2. How much of the blend does Petit
    Verdot account for?

    A. 1-3%

    B. 15-35%

    C. 40-48%

3. Petit Verdot has leather and violet
    aromas, however when young, which
    fruit aromas do they give off?

    A. Apple

    B. Banana

    C. Pineapple

4. True or false? In Peru, the desert
    weather allows producers to make
    100% varietal Petit Verdot wines.

5. Petit Verdot is normally a blend, however, if a varietal is made, it is best after being aged for how long?

A. 5 years

B. 8 years

C. 10 years

PINOT BLANC

1. Pinot Blanc is a white wine grape. True or false? Pinot Blanc is classed as a point mutation of Pinot Noir. This is where a vine produces all black fruit except for one cane which produces white fruit.

2. Which style of wines are usually produced by this grape variety?

    A. Light bodied

    B. Medium bodied

    C. Full bodied

3. True or false? Pinot Blanc is the most grown grape variety in the French wine region of Alsace.

4. True or false? Pinot Blanc is the signature wine for the Okanagan Valley region of Canada.

5. What are the typical aromas of a Pinot

Blanc wine?

A. Apple and citrus fruit

B. Pineapple and starfruit

C. Gooseberry and passion fruit

PINOT GRIGIO

1. True or false? Pinot Grigio and Pinot Gris are the same grape variety.

2. Which type of wine is produced from the Pinot Grigio grape?

    A. Red wine

    B. Port style wine

    C. White wine

3. What is the ideal serving temperature for Pinot Grigio wine?

    A. 5 □C

    B. 7 □C

    C. 9 □C

4. Pinot Grigio is planted all around the world. True or false? Pinot Grigio is most planted in the USA than any other country.

5. True or false? German Pinot Grigio is full bodied, USA Pinot Grigio is medium bodied and Italian Pinot Grigio is light bodied.

PINOT NOIR

1. True or false? Pinot Noir is one of the three main varieties used in the production of Champagne.

2. What is the ideal serving temperature of Pinot Noir?

   A. 13-15 □C

   B. 15-17 □C

   C. 17-19 □C

3. True or false? More Pinot Noir is grown in the USA than in France.

4. A Pinot Noir wine typically has which fruit flavours?

   A. Strawberry, Raspberry, Plum

   B. Black Cherry, Blackberry, Blueberry

   C. Cranberry, Cherry, Raspberry

5. True or false? Pinot Noir is the second

most widely planted grape variety in the United Kingdom.

PORT

1. What type of wine is Port?

    A. Red wine

    B. Dessert wine

    C. Fortified wine

2. A typical Port wine contains which level of alcohol?

    A. 15-17%

    B. 19-20%

    C. 20-22%

3. In which European country is Port exclusively produced?

4. True or false? Strawberry, Raspberry, Cranberry Sauce and Caramel are common flavours of Tawny Port.

5. Rosé Port is ideally served at which temperature?

A. 4 □C

B. 12 □C

C. 16□C

RETSINA

1. Retsina is from which European country?

2. True or false? Retsina can be White or Rosé wine.

3. What is Retsina flavoured with?

4. Which grape variety is primarily used for producing Retsina?

    A. Savatiano

    B. Robola

    C. Debina

5. True or false? Retsina wine production can be traced back as far as the 2nd Century.

ROSÉ

1. The most common method of producing Rosé wine is by skin contact. How long is the grape skin left in the pressed grape juice during production?

    A. 1-3 days

    B. 5-7 days

    C. 14-21 days

2. France is the largest Rosé wine producing country in the world. How much of the world's Rosé wine does France produce?

    A. 19%

    B. 28%

    C. 43%

3. After France, which country is the 2nd largest consumer of Rosé wine?

    A. USA

B. Canada

C. Australia

4. True or false? Like Red wines, Rosé wines can improve flavours and aromas by ageing/cellaring for 5 years or more.

5. Rosé wine is best served at which temperature?

A. 4-6 ☐C

B. 6-9 ☐C

C. 10-15 ☐C

SANGIOVESE

1. True or false? In Italy, Sangiovese is the most planted red wine grape?

2. What are the typical flavours of a Sangiovese wine?

   A. Raspberry, Blackberry, Blueberry

   B. Black cherry, Liquorice, Plum

   C. Tart Cherry, Red plum, Strawberry

3. True or false? Chianti wines must be made with at least 85% Sangiovese.

4. The world-famous Brunello di Montalcino is made from 100% Sangiovese. How long is it aged in oak barrels?

   A. 3 years

   B. 5 years

   C. 7 years

5. Which style of wine is Brunello di Montalcino?

A. Light bodied

B. Medium bodied

C. Full bodied

SAUTERNES

1. Which type of wine is Sauternes?

    A. Dry

    B. Medium

    C. Sweet

2. What is the minimum level of alcohol content a Sauternes wine must have?

    A. 12%

    B. 13%

    C. 14%

3. True or false? A Sauternes wine typically starts out golden in colour and darkens to an almost copper colour as it ages.

4. In which French wine region mainly notable for its red wines is Sauternes wine produced?

A. Bordeaux

B. Beaujolais

C. Burgundy

5. What are the typical flavours of a Sauternes wine?

A. Apricots, Honey, Peaches

B. Gooseberry, Pear, Apple

C. Water melon, Fig, Citrus

SAUVIGNON BLANC

1. True or false? Sauvignon Blanc that has not been aged in oak should be served at 8 □C and oak aged Sauvignon Blanc should be served at 11 □C.

2. How does the Sauvignon Blanc grape rank in the world's most planted varieties?

   A. 3rd

   B. 5th

   C. 8th

3. True or false? The Sauvignon Blanc grape variety is older than the Cabernet Sauvignon grape variety.

4. Sauvignon Blanc can produce varietal and blended wines. Which other grape variety is commonly blended with Sauvignon Blanc to produce White Bordeaux wines?

5. In which decade did Sauvignon Blanc wines from New Zealand first become popular on the international wine market?

A. 1970's

B. 1980's

C. 1990's

SHERRY

1. Which type of wine is Sherry?

    A. Fortified wine

    B. Dessert wine

    C. White wine

2. How many grape varieties are used for producing Sherry?

    A. 2

    B. 3

    C. 5

3. Which type of oak barrels is Sherry aged in?

    A. North American oak

    B. French oak

    C. Spanish oak

4. Which level of alcohol content does an

"Oloroso Sherry" typically have?

A. 13-15%

B. 15-17%

C. 18-22%

5. In which country is Sherry produced?

A. Portugal

B. Spain

C. United Kingdom

SOAVE

1. Which type of wine is Soave?

    A. White wine

    B. Red wine

    C. Dessert wine

2. Which Italian wine region is Soave from?

    A. Sardinia

    B. Tuscany

    C. Veneto

3. What is the primary grape variety used for producing Soave?

    A. Garganega

    B. Catarratto

    C. Malvasia Bianca

4. What are the most common flavours of

Soave wine?

A. Ripe pineapple and baked apple

B. Peach and honeydew melon

C. Pear and starfruit

5. How much of the primary grape (answer number 3) must a Soave wine contain?

A. 70%

B. 80%

C. 85%

TREBBIANO

1. True or false? Trebbiano is the 2nd most planted grape variety in the world.

2. What is Trebbiano known as in France?

3. In Italy, as well as white wine, what other product is produced from Trebbiano grapes?

4. In France, what is primarily produced using Trebbiano Grapes?

5. Trebbiano grapes are used to produce Orvieto Italian wine. Which style of wine is Orvieto?

   A. Sweet and light bodied

   B. Dry and medium bodied

   C. Sweet and medium bodied

VALPOLICELLA

1. Which type of wine is Valpolicella?

    A. White wine

    B. Fortified wine

    C. Red wine

2. How many styles of Valpolicella wine are there?

    A. 3

    B. 5

    C. 7

3. A Valpolicella Classico (an everyday style) is typically light bodied with cherry notes. What level of alcohol do these typically contain?

    A. 8-9%

    B. 10-11%

C. 11-12%

4. A Valpolicella Superiore must have a minimum alcohol content of 12% and must also be aged in wood for a minimum amount of time. How long is the minimum ageing time?

   A. 1 year

   B. 3 years

   C. 5 years

5. True or false? Amarone della Valpolicella wine is made from grapes that have been dried for 6-9 months.

VIOGNIER

1. Which style of wine is produced by the Viognier grape variety?

   A. Light bodied

   B. Medium bodied

   C. Full bodied

2. True or false? Viognier grapes are used to make red and white wines?

3. The Viognier grape is the only variety allowed to be used for producing which Rhône Valley wine?

   A. Condrieu

   B. Chablis

   C. Pouilly-Fuissé

4. Viognier wines typically have which level of alcohol content?

   A. 11-12.5%

B. 13.5-15%

C. 15-16%

5. Viognier vines start to hit their peak after 15-20 years. True or false? In the Rhône Valley there are Viognier vines at least 100 years old.

ZINFANDEL

1. What is Zinfandel also known as?

2. True or false? The USA grows the most Zinfandel in the world.

3. What is the ideal serving temperature for Zinfandel?

    A. 16 □C

    B. 17 □C

    C. 18 □C

4. The alcohol content of red Zinfandel can be 13.5-17%. What level of alcohol content does a white Zinfandel typically have?

    A. 9-10%

    B. 10-13%

    C. 13-16%

5. True or false? 85% of total Zinfandel

production is white Zinfandel.

TOP 10 MOST PLANTED WINE GRAPE VARIETIES

Arrange these grape varieties in order of most planted to least planted

1. Airen

2. Sauvignon Blanc

3. Grenache

4. Cabernet Sauvignon

5. Pinot Noir

6. Chardonnay

7. Merlot

8. Syrah

9. Tempranillo

10. Trebbiano

TOP 10 WINE PRODUCING COUNTRIES

Arrange these countries in order of wine production (greatest to least)

1. Germany

2. Chile

3. Spain

4. Italy

5. China

6. France

7. USA

8. Argentina

9. South Africa

10. Australia

117

QUIZ ANSWERS
ALBARIÑO

1. Alvarinho or Cainho Branco

2. 11.5-12.5%

3. True

4. Apricot and Peach

5. True

ALIGOTÉ

1. White wine

2. 18th

3. False

4. 2nd

5. Apples and Lemons

AMARONE

119

1. Amarone della Valpolicella

2. Red wine

3. 14%

4. True

5. "The great bitter"

ARNEIS

1. Piedmont

2. White wine

3. Dry and full bodied

4. Gisborne

5. Pears and apricots

ASTI SPUMANTE

1. Sparkling wine

2. Piedmont

3. Moscato Bianco

4. Varietal

5. 7-9.5%

AUSLESE

1. Selected harvest

2. Dessert wine

3. 13-14%

4. 10 years or more

5. 7%

BANYULS

1. Dessert wine

2. 15%

3. 10 months

4. Blend

5. False, it's light to medium bodied with dark cherry, raisin and cocoa flavours

BARBARESCO

1. 45%

2. 12.5%

3. Varietal

4. 2 years (1 in oak)

5. Cherry and liquorice

BARDOLINO

1. Red wine

2. Molinara

3. Veneto

4. True

5. 15%

BAROLO

1. Nebbiolo

2. 13%

3. 60 months (18 months in oak)

4. Full bodied

5. False, it's the bark from the Cinchona tree

BEAUJOLAIS

1. True

2. 1%

3. Chardonnay

4. False, it's the 3rd Thursday

5. 1/3

BRUNELLO di MONTALCINO

1. True

2. Tuscany

3. Red wine

4. Minimum 2 years in a barrel and 4 months in the bottle

5. Full bodied

CABERNET FRANC

1. True

2. 4th

3. True

4. 12-18 months

5. False, it's Cabernet Franc and Sauvignon Blanc

CABERNET SAUVIGNON

1. Full bodied

2. False, it's usually aged for 9-18 months

3. 13.5-15.5%

4. 60%

5. True

CARMÉNÈRE

1. True

2. Chile

3. Raspberry and pomegranate

4. False, it's allowed up to 15%

5. True

CAVA

1. Sparkling wine

2. 30 months

3. Sweet

4. True

5. 95%

CHAMPAGNE

1. Up to 50,000 bottles

2. Chardonnay

3. True

4. Pinot Noir and Pinot Meunier

5. Blanc de blanc (white from white)

CHARDONNAY

1. White wine

2. False, it's Ugni blanc

3. 12-15%

4. 9 □C

5. True

CHÂTEAUNEUF-du-PAPE

1. Rhône

2. True

3. Grenache

4. 16

5. 12.5%

CHENIN BLANC

1. True

2. Loire

3. 1/5

4. True

5. False, the 1st harvests produce sparkling and dry wines

CHIANTI

1. Sangiovese

2. 75-100%

3. 15 □C

4. 11.5%

5. Tuscany

CONSTANTIA

1. Dessert wine

2. South Africa

3. Muscat Blanc à Petits Grains

4. True

5. Greece

CORTESE

1. Piedmont

2. Medium bodied

3. White wine

4. Lime and greengage

5. Fish

DOLCETTO

1. "Little sweet one"

2. Red wine

3. Black cherry and liquorice

4. Pasta and pizza

5. 12.5%

DURIF

1. France

2. True

3. Red wine

4. True

5. 14-15%

EISWEIN

1. Dessert wine

2. True

3. False, they are hand picked

4. 75%

5. 8-13%

GAMAY

1. True

2. Light bodied

3. Strawberry and raspberry

4. False

5. 13 □C

GATTINARA

1. Red wine

2. Piedmont

3. Nebbiolo

4. 90%

5. 2 years in oak barrels and 2 years in the bottle

GEWÜRZTRAMINER

1. True

2. Lychee

3. Alsace

4. 6 □C

5. Asian cuisine

GRENACHE

1. Red wine

2. At least 15%

3. False, Merlot is the most common

4. Cannonau

5. True

LAMBRUSCO

1. Sparkling wine

2. 5.5%

3. 11%

4. False, most Lambrusco wines are blended

5. Secco

LIEBFRAUMILCH

1. White wine

2. True

3. Beloved lady's milk

4. Semi-sweet

5. False, it's for export

MADEIRA

1. 20 years

2. Rosé wine

3. True

4. Sercial, Verdelho, Bual, Malmsey

5. Portugal

MALBEC

1. Red wine

2. True

3. Full bodied

4. 21 □C

5. A + B

MARSALA

1. False, it's also a sipping wine like Sherry or Madeira

2. Sicily

3. 15-20%

4. At least 4 years

5. 13 □C

MARSANNE

1. Varietal and blended

2. True

3. France

4. Full bodied

5. 15%

MERLOT

1. False

2. True

3. Red wine

4. False, it was the Chilean wine industry

5. Black Cherry, Raspberry, Plum

MOURVÈDRE

1. Spain

2. Full bodied

3. Châteauneuf-du-Pape

4. False, typical flavours are Blueberry, Blackberry, Plum

5. True

NEBBIOLO

1. Italy

2. True

3. Full bodied

4. 95%

5. 20 months (6 months in wooden barrels)

PETIT VERDOT

1. True

2. 1-3%

3. Banana

4. True

5. 5 years

PINOT BLANC

1. True

2. Full bodied

3. False

4. True

5. Apple and citrus fruits

PINOT GRIGIO

1. True

2. White wine

3. 7 °C

4. False, it's most planted in Italy

5. True

PINOT NOIR

1. True

2. 13-15 °C

3. False

4. Cranberry, Cherry, Raspberry

5. True

PORT

1. Fortified wine

2. 19-20%

3. Portugal

4. False, it's Caramel, Raspberry, Hazelnut, Cinnamon, Clove and Fig

5. 4 °C

RETSINA

1. Greece

2. True

3. Pine resin

4. Savatiano

5. True

ROSÉ

1. 1-3 days

2. 28%

3. USA

4. False, Rosé should be consumed within 2-3 years of purchase at the longest

5. 10-15 □C

SANGIOVESE

1. True

2. Tart Cherry, Red plum, Strawberry

3. False, they must be made with at least 70% Sangiovese

4. 3 years

5. Full bodied

SAUTERNES

1. Sweet wine

2. 13%

3. True

4. Bordeaux

5. Apricots, Honey, Peaches

SAUVIGNON BLANC

1. True

2. 8th

3. True

4. Sémillon

5. 1990's

SHERRY

1. Fortified wine

2. 3

3. North American oak

4. 18-22%

5. Spain

SOAVE

1. White wine

2. Veneto

3. Garganega

4. Peach and honeydew melon

5. 70%

TREBBIANO

1. True

2. Ugni Blanc

3. Balsamic vinegar

4. Cognac

5. Dry and medium bodied

VALPOLICELLA

1. Red wine

2. 5

3. 11-12%

4. 1 year

5. False, they are dried for 4-5 months in special drying rooms

VIOGNIER

1. Full bodied

2. True

3. Condrieu

4. 13.5-15%

5. False, there are vines at least 70 years old

ZINFANDEL

1. Primitivo

2. True

3. 17 □C

4. 9-10%

5. True

TOP 10 MOST PLANTED WINE GRAPE VARIETIES

1. Cabernet Sauvignon

2. Merlot

3. Tempranillo

4. Airen

5. Chardonnay

6. Syrah

7. Grenache Noir

8. Sauvignon Blanc

9. Pinot Noir

10. Trebbiano

TOP 10 WINE PRODUCING COUNTRIES

1. Italy

2. France

3. USA

4. Spain

5. Australia

6. Argentina

7. China

8. South Africa

9. Chile

10. Germany

All questions and answers are correct at the time of writing. August 2022 (revised).

150